About the British Institute of Learning Disabilities

The British Institute of Learning Disabilities is committed to improving the quality of life for people with a learning disability by involving them and their families in all aspects of our work, working with government and public bodies to achieve full citizenship, undertaking beneficial research and development projects and helping service providers to develop and share good practice.

Acknowledgements

BILD remains grateful to the large number of organisations and individuals, both local and national, who contributed to the first edition of the Code of Practice in 2001. BILD would like to express thanks to members of BILD accredited training organisations, assessors of the BILD accreditation scheme, Physical Intervention Accreditation panel members and commissioners of training for their contributions to this edition. Thanks are also extended to the Department for Education and Skills for providing the funding to enable the revision to take place, and to Ann Hunt, David Leadbetter, Brodie Paterson and Sharon Paley who undertook the development.

Contents

Introduction

The original BILD Code of Practice was produced in 2001 by the British Institute of Learning Disabilities in response to requests to clarify the standards of training available following the publication of statutory and regulatory guidance in the field of physical intervention. This revised edition endeavours to take account of further developments in the field and to recognise the importance of an overall framework of good practice in the use of physical interventions and the raft of preventive measures that are used beforehand.

The Code is designed for use by trainers in their planning processes and by commissioning organisations looking for appropriate and accredited training in any setting where there are children, young people or adults with:

- a learning disability
- an autistic spectrum condition
- a special educational need (both those with statements and those without)
- severe behavioural, emotional and social difficulties

Preventive strategies should be developed in all settings for people who use services in order to support them and manage challenging behaviours. It is important for employers, staff and individuals alike that these strategies emanate from well-thought-out policies, with support plans containing a gradient of preventive measures to diffuse difficult situations, the last resort being physical interventions. It is equally important that staff have access to appropriate training in order to put agreed policies and plans into practice when necessary.

The Code aims to set out clear expectations and standards of training for all users. It should be read in conjunction with existing legislation, associated guidance and other relevant BILD guidance (a reference list is included at the end of this guide).

NB: This edition of the Code contains references to relevant Scottish legislation and good practice guides published by the Scottish Executive. Some of the descriptors (classifications and definitions) used in this edition are no longer in use in Scotland and have in some cases been replaced by new terms and concepts. Some of these terms are not interchangeable so readers in Scotland will need to take care when using this document.

Why is a code of practice needed?

The Code not only clarifies expected standards of training but helps to ensure that physical interventions are part of a wider strategy of dealing with challenging behaviours and are only used in appropriate circumstances to minimise the risk of injury or distress to people who use services, staff and members of the public. By providing explicit statements about the commissioning and delivery of this training, it is hoped the Code will be a point of reference for both commissioners of training and those responsible for its delivery.

Assistance for commissioners of training will help to produce better informed decision-making in respect of:

- the kind of training that is appropriate to meet the needs of specific groups of people who use services
- how training in physical interventions should be integrated with other training in the field of preventing socially invalid behaviours, supporting people and managing challenging behaviours
- which staff and how many should be included in a training session
- the quantity and content of training required for staff working in different settings and supporting different individuals
- the structure, content and frequency of follow-up or refresher training
- the choice of training provider, based on the individual needs of the service and the children, young people or adults who use that service

Assistance for training providers will include:

- greater consistency in the approach to training in physical interventions
- higher standards of training
- assistance in highlighting the responsibilities of the commissioners of training
- support and guidance in developing service-specific training

Physical interventions training organisations that implement and demonstrate adherence to the standards of the Code can be awarded BILD accreditation. The BILD accreditation scheme is now well established and it is hoped it will lead to the following benefits for trainers:

- widespread agreement in the way in which training should be commissioned and delivered
- increased clarity between trainers and commissioners regarding their respective responsibilities in commissioning and delivering training
- closer collaboration between service provider organisations and schools in the trainers they employ
- improved training outcomes
- increased staff skills and confidence in the use of physical interventions
- fewer injuries to staff and people who use services when physical interventions are used
- a greater understanding by staff that physical intervention is the last resort in behaviour management techniques
- a reduction in the use of physical interventions to manage challenging behaviour

Putting the Code into practice

The BILD Code of Practice represents a consensus statement from all those consulted about good practice in commissioning and delivering training on physical interventions. Included in the consultation process were NHS Trusts, local authority social services departments, independent and voluntary sector service providers, staff working in special and mainstream schools and colleges, members of the Commission for Social Care Inspection, commissioners in the health service, social services and education departments and many trainers who teach approaches to physical intervention to staff working with children and adults in a wide range of settings.

Trainers and training organisations wishing to apply for BILD accreditation are expected to undertake the following procedure:

- submit an expression of interest in further pursuing accreditation
- attend a formal induction workshop
- demonstrate practice that reflects adherence to the Code and relevant national guidance
- submit a written document identifying how the training organisation meets the criteria for accreditation (that are based on the Code)
- make an oral presentation to the accreditation panel

Commissioners of training are encouraged to use individual trainers or training organisations who have been successfully accredited. An up-to-date list of accredited organisations is maintained on the BILD website (www.bild.org.uk). Commissioners are also encouraged to make reference to *Guidance for Restrictive Physical Interventions* (DoH/DfES, 2002).

Any organisation or individual having concerns that an accredited trainer is not operating according to the standards and procedures set out in the Code should pass on these concerns in writing to BILD. BILD should also be informed of any organisation that states it is accredited but does not appear on the website.

In revising the Code in 2006 BILD continues to emphasise the need for a comprehensive framework which ensures that physical interventions are reasonable, appropriate and proportionate in the circumstances and only used:

- in the best interest of the people who use services
- in ways that maintain the safety and dignity of all concerned
- when less intrusive approaches have been tried and proved unsuccessful

The BILD Code of Practice

The Code has been developed in response to an identified need to establish quality and consistency of training in the use of physical interventions. By raising standards of training the Code will improve the quality of service available to individuals who may experience physical interventions. These are adults, young people and children who have:

- a learning disability
- an autistic spectrum condition
- special educational needs
- severe behavioural, emotional and social difficulties

The Code is intended for use by training organisations and trainers in physical interventions, and those who commission training from them. Its development was carried out after consultation with:

- representatives of training organisations
- schools and providers of services for adults and children with learning disabilities and autistic spectrum conditions
- Department of Health (DoH)
- Department for Education and Skills (DfES)
- Health and Safety Executive (HSE)
- Nursing and Midwifery Council (NMC)

Training that conforms to this Code will help:

- learning disability services and schools to meet the requirements of the *Guidance for Restrictive Physical Interventions* (2002) issued by DoH and DfES
- services and schools to work within the legislation on health and safety at work
- professionals in the field to meet their professional commitments (eg nurses and the NMC Code of Conduct)
- teachers in a variety of school settings to recognise appropriate actions to take when supporting pupils and preventing and managing challenging behaviour

Widespread support for the Code and BILD accreditation scheme will lead to:

- a more consistent approach throughout the UK to training staff in the use of physical interventions
- increasing numbers of staff who understand the contexts in which physical interventions would be judged to be appropriate and legal, and who are trained and supported to use them
- clear expectations among the agencies commissioning the training about the quality of training they expect
- improved standards of training

These benefits will in turn help services and schools to deliver higher standards of care, support and education in respect of:

- compliance with health and safety regulations
- services that are safe for people who use services and staff
- improved quality of care for children and vulnerable adults who display socially invalid behaviours that present significant risk to them or others and may experience physical interventions

The BILD Code of Practice should be read in conjunction with the joint BILD and National Autistic Society (NAS) document *Physical Interventions: A Policy Framework*, published by BILD. It is also important to make reference to the joint *Guidance for Restrictive Physical Interventions* (2002).

1 Policies

1.1 Trainers delivering courses on physical interventions should make reference to the following considerations that are intended to achieve a balance between protecting the rights of people who use services and of the staff supporting them:

- the legal and professional framework, the duty of care, and health and safety requirements that apply in the workplace (NB: Health and safety legislation applies across the UK, but some other aspects of the law in Scotland differ from the rest of the UK)
- the values base set out in the joint BILD and National Autistic Society (NAS) policy framework
- the BILD physical interventions accreditation scheme
- organisational policies on the management of challenging behaviour that apply to course participants in their workplace
- organisational policies on the management of physical interventions that apply to course participants in their workplace
- the principles of least restrictive physical intervention and minimum use of force
- good practice in developing individual support plans and reviewing the support needs of people who use services
- the importance of systematic monitoring of the use of physical interventions and procedures to protect the best interests of people who use services
- the rights of people who use services to be consulted on the use of strategies and interventions that affect them (in Scotland this is a requirement)
- the influence of staff attitudes and service culture, and the importance of addressing attitudes during training
- the entitlement of staff to training in physical interventions
- the right of staff to take reasonable action to defend themselves in accordance with the law and the obligation of organisations and schools to provide appropriate training under HSE regulations

- policies dealing with the care of staff, including those in respect of child protection and health and safety at work
- the importance of not sharing physical intervention skills informally

1.2 To ensure that staff training links directly with organisational policies, trainers should take all possible steps to:

- arrange a meeting between all relevant agencies, including where appropriate people who use services, their carers and families. This should be in the presence of the person responsible for delivering the training in the organisation or school and should include discussion on policies relating to the use of physical interventions in different settings.
- provide pre-training briefing sessions for managers and staff to address:
  - health and safety within the context of physical interventions
  - the responsibilities of commissioning organisations within the BILD Code of Practice
  - sector specific guidance from relevant government departments in the four UK countries
- tailor training programmes to match variations in organisational policies
- review organisational training policies at regular intervals and where necessary advise on their revision in the light of what is learned during training
- in the case of external trainers, remind the commissioning agency in writing of their responsibilities with regard to policy development and implementation
- ensure that monitoring and reporting on the use of physical interventions comply with all statutory duties, and that lines of accountability are clear to all concerned

2 Best interest criteria

2.1 Training in the use of physical interventions should be provided only in conjunction with training in:

- risk assessment and risk management
- the role of individual support plans and individual educational plans with a behaviour support component that highlights primary and secondary preventions strategies
- strategies for promoting alternative behaviours that provide a functional equivalent to the socially invalid behaviours
- behaviour assessment and understanding of functional aspects of behaviour for people
- alternative methods of responding to aggressive and violent behaviour
- multidisciplinary assessment and review in planning intervention strategies
- the prevention of violence, aggression and other unsafe or high-risk behaviours

2.2 Trainers should provide training on physical intervention techniques solely to organisations and schools that demonstrate, or confirm in writing, that they have implemented policies and practices in the areas identified in 2.1 above.

2.3 Trainers should ensure that the commissioning organisation has developed and implemented appropriate health procedures for confirming, prior to the training, the fitness of staff to participate.

2.4 Trainers should discuss with commissioning organisations, and advise them in writing, of course participants who may require additional training or development as a result of the characteristics of their working environment or of the individuals with whom they work. This should also take place in respect of any physical or health-related issues.

2.5 If trainers have concerns about the competence or conduct of any participants during training they should inform them of this and if necessary exclude them from the course. Excluded participants should be informed that these concerns will be conveyed in writing to senior managers in the employing organisation.

2.6 Training should include:

- an overview of the *Guidance for Restrictive Physical Interventions* and *BILD Code of Practice*
- an overview of relevant national guidance and legislation
- the development of an understanding of the importance of an appropriate values base for working with individuals that may require physical interventions
- an understanding of cultural issues that may affect the use of physical contact by staff working with individuals from different ethnic backgrounds
- an understanding of gender issues that may affect the use of physical contact, and the need to avoid contact with sexual areas
- the relevance of age and age-related issues (that may need to take account of developmental issues in services for people with learning disabilities or autism)
- the assessment of individuals for any health condition that would place them at risk in the event of a physical intervention being used
- the common contraindications for the use of physical interventions
- the difference between 'escorting',' touching' and' 'holding' (eg the main factors separating 'holding' from 'physical restraint' are the manner of intervention, the degree of force applied and the motivation) *Guidance for Restrictive Physical Interventions* (2002)

- the use of gradients of control and support to implement the principles of minimum force and minimum duration
- the avoidance of potentially dangerous postures and positioning, with reference to ergonomic, physiological and biomechanical factors
- the known mechanisms of restraint-related injury and fatality (eg positional asphyxia, etc)
- reference to high risk strategies as defined in section 3 of the *Guidance for Restrictive Physical Interventions*
- the importance of developing individual support or behaviour plans for people who use services that describe agreed methods of intervention, including the use of reactive physical interventions as a planned response
- the monitoring of an individual's physical well-being while physical interventions are employed
- procedures for assessment of an individual following the use of a physical intervention
- physical care, including how to summon help and the appropriate course of action in the event of accidental injury in the workplace while physical interventions are being used
- the provision of psychological support for individuals and staff following the use of physical intervention (which should be done with reference to post incident debrief and support)
- systematic review of the outcomes associated with the use of physical interventions

Training should also include clear advice on the relevance and necessity of recording all incidents that involve the use of physical interventions.

2.7 Training should reflect the principles that any use of physical intervention will:

- be considered only when all other methods have been examined and judged to be ineffective

- be used as a last resort
- employ the minimum reasonable amount of force
- be used for the shortest possible time
- form part of an individual care and support plan, but for the shortest possible period, and subject to regular review at not less than three-monthly intervals

2.8 Training should be tailored to meet the needs and abilities of:

- the course participants, taking into account factors such as age, strength and gender
- the individuals who are likely to need physical interventions
- the characteristics of the commissioning organisation or school, including its philosophy, mission statement, policy on the management of challenging behaviour, and staffing levels

2.9 Employers are legally responsible for arranging refresher courses for their staff. Trainers should work in partnership with employers and managers such as executive boards for Trusts, school governors, local education authorities and managers to facilitate refresher courses and to ensure that staff skills are maintained at a level that is appropriate to their working environment.

3 Techniques for physical intervention

3.1 Trainers should ask service provider organisations and schools to carry out an audit of all physically challenging behaviours presented by the people who use their services. This should be sent to the training provider at least two weeks prior to the training.

3.2 In describing their course, trainers should specify in writing the intervention techniques that involve the use of restrictive physical interventions.

3.3 In consultation with the trainer, the commissioning organisation or school should provide a clear statement in writing of the rationale for these techniques based upon the audit and their relevance to:

- adults and children with a learning disability
- adults and children with autistic spectrum conditions
- pupils with special educational needs
- children with severe behavioural, emotional and social disorders

3.4 Training should include only physical interventions that comply with national policy guidance, comply with section 3.7 of the joint DoH/DfES *Guidance for Restrictive Physical Interventions,* and that are based on best available evidence or research and in accordance with the risk assessments completed by the accredited training organisations as part of the BILD Physical Interventions Accreditation Scheme. This means techniques taught should:

- be appropriate for use with adults and children with a learning disability or autistic spectrum disorders, pupils with special educational needs and children with emotional and behavioural difficulties

- not impede the process of breathing
- not inflict pain or be developed with pain compliance as an effective component of the techniques taught
- avoid vulnerable parts of the body (eg neck, chest and sexual areas)
- avoid hyperextension and hyperflexion
- not employ potentially dangerous positions, for example positions that may compromise breathing or the welfare and safety of the person based upon their individual characteristics and profile (which must be considered in the context of all relevant individual risk assessments)
- provide clear guidance on the importance of using each technique as taught and not attempt unsupervised modifications

3.5 Physical interventions taught to staff should be appropriate to their workplace and its service users. Training in these interventions should prepare staff for their use in both predictable incidents and in response to unforeseeable circumstances. Trainers should specifically refer to sections 3.8, 3.9 and 3.10 of the *Guidance for Restrictive Physical Interventions.*

3.6 Additional techniques to meet the specific needs of individuals who use services, for example those set out in section 3.7 of the *Guidance for Restrictive Physical Interventions,* should be taught only in exceptional circumstances and where the trainer has clearly established that:

- documentation demonstrates alternative strategies have been unsuccessful
- the identified service user's particular support requirements indicate the need
- an individual behavioural support plan, including positive behavioural strategies, is in place

- the behaviours that cause concern are identified and an assessment of associated risks has occurred
- there exists an explicit rationale for the use of individualised physical intervention procedures
- regular reviews of support plans are provided for

3.7 In services for people who have learning disabilities or autistic spectrum disorders, and for children who have behavioural difficulties or special educational needs, and where staff are providing support through person-centred approaches, techniques that cause pain or discomfort pose major ethical and moral difficulties. They may also be difficult to apply with the appropriate care and skill. They are:

- damaging to the therapeutic relationship between care staff and service user
- liable to be abused or improperly used

Morally and ethically BILD is opposed to the use of touching, guiding or holding techniques that might or are known to cause pain or discomfort, or techniques that are designed to use pain as an effective component to gain compliance, and believes the presumption must be that they are not to be taught.

3.8 Trainers who are asked to teach additional techniques that might cause pain or discomfort should ask the commissioning organisation to consider all the factors that are raised in sections 3.6 and 3.7 of this Code, or are detailed in section 3.7 of the *Guidance for Restrictive Physical Interventions* (2002), together with the following points:

- the moral obligation to undertake wide consultation, prior to the use of such additional techniques, including with the service user concerned so far as he or she is competent to give consent, and with the service user's family and advocates, on a similar basis to that required when intrusive medical treatment is being considered, and with a view to establishing a consensus on the service user's best interests

- the likelihood that with the necessary commitment and resources an alternative pain-free method can be developed to achieve at least essential outcomes in the best interests of the individual service user and others
- the necessity to have a robust risk assessment in relation to the target behaviour and the described planned physical intervention technique that should make reference to an individual behaviour support plan and detail the alternative behaviour support strategies that are in place to drive down the frequency of the target behaviour
- the difficulties and resource implications associated with establishing and maintaining sufficiently high standards of training among sufficient numbers of staff to be able to provide a safe and consistent service in applying such techniques when appropriate
- the difficulties that may arise after the use of such techniques of justifying specific actions in terms of the *Guidance for Restrictive Physical Interventions*, other relevant departmental guidance and the law

3.9 At the end of the training course participants' competence to use physical interventions should be systematically evaluated to determine:

- how successfully individual participants have learned the appropriate skills and underpinning knowledge
- whether any participant has failed to acquire the necessary skills and knowledge to employ physical interventions safely and effectively

3.10 At the completion of a training course the commissioning agency is responsible for evaluating itself or for ensuring that the trainer concerned evaluates the ability of course participants to apply their learning to situations they are likely to encounter in the workplace.

4 Health and safety

Before training

4.1 Those attending courses that include instruction on practical techniques for physical intervention should receive clear information, at least two weeks before the start of the course, regarding the physical requirements for course participants. This information should indicate that the commissioner of training, not the trainer, is responsible for the occupational health of the course participants. Advice should also be included on appropriate clothing and footwear, and guidance on the securing of hair and removal of jewellery before undertaking training in physical interventions.

It is the responsibility of the commissioning organisation to assess all participants to ensure that they are fit to participate in training and to confirm this to the trainer. Where this is not done, the trainer should require participants to complete a health questionnaire as evidence that they can undertake training safely.

Employees should be reminded that they have a legal obligation to report any factors that could increase the risk they face in the workplace. These include physical conditions such as pregnancy, heart conditions or brittle bones, and also personal circumstances.

During training

4.2 Trainers should remind course participants of the risk assessment procedures of their own organisation and their personal responsibilities in relation to:

- guarding against the risk of injury during training and immediately reporting any subsequent injury to the trainers
- reporting existing injuries and disabilities that pose health and safety risks

- their own safety and welfare and those of other course participants during training
- reporting all injuries or adverse events in accordance with statutory guidance, (eg Health and Safety Executive (HSE), Reporting of Injuries, Diseases and Dangerous Occurrences Regulations (RIDDOR) and Care Standards) to the commissioning organisation, including any sustained during training

4.3 Any course participant who is unsure of his or her capacity to undertake training on physical techniques safely should be offered a personal risk assessment by an experienced occupational health practitioner or doctor by the commissioning organisation.

4.4 The trainer has the right to exclude from the course anyone who he or she believes to be unsuitable for training on the basis of health, physical status or attitude. Any such exclusion should be subsequently confirmed to the commissioner in writing. The employing organisation retains responsibility for the health and safety of employees throughout the training course.

4.5 Training should take place in a safe and suitable environment. There must be sufficient space to avoid danger from obstacles such as furniture and fittings. When participants are required to kneel, sit or lie on the floor, the surface must be covered with a suitable gym mat or equivalent covering in order to provide greater comfort and protection from possible injuries.

4.6 Participants should be required to undertake gentle and appropriate mobilisation activities as directed by the trainer to ensure that they are adequately prepared to engage in the training activities.

4.7 It is good practice for trainers to work in pairs. The ratio of trainers to course participants should not exceed 1:12.

4.8 In exceptional circumstances, for example where there are overriding concerns for the safety of staff or people who use the services, larger groups may be taught. Where this is necessary there should be a written agreement between the training and commissioning organisations that sets out:

- the reasons for working in a larger group
- the limitations this imposes on the training programme
- additional concerns regarding health and safety during training and how identified risks will be overcome
- agreement on what limitations the larger group will have on group management and the assessment of performance
- details of any training that is required to ensure appropriate levels of competence among course participants, with the possibility of more frequent refresher training
- arrangements for follow-up training to take place as soon as possible – where practicable within 6 months

4.9 Trainers should hold an appropriate and up-to-date first aid qualification to enable them to respond to injuries that might arise during training. A minimum requirement for trainers is that they have attended a one-day emergency first aid course. If trainers do not have this appropriate first aid qualification themselves they should make arrangements for someone else with the appropriate first aid qualification to be available during training sessions. First aiders should be on site so that they can respond quickly, but not necessarily in the same building. Trainers must ensure that suitable first aid facilities and equipment are readily accessible at the training venue. Trainers should also know how to summon emergency services from the venue should a serious injury occur during a training session.

4.10 All training organisations, their trainers and instructors should be covered by professional indemnity and public liability insurance. Copies of a current certificate of insurance should be made available to commissioning agencies.

4.11 Commissioning organisations that employ physical intervention instructors or that run training on their own premises should ensure that their insurance specifically covers this activity.

5 Course organisation

5.1 Commissioning organisations are responsible for the following areas of training course organisation:

- selecting suitable course participants, based on attitudes towards people with a learning disability or an autistic spectrum disorder, or individuals with special educational needs or emotional and social behavioural difficulties. Selection should also be based on knowledge of the principles underpinning good practice in the management of challenging behaviours.
- providing the chosen participants with advance written information about the training course.
- advising their organisation's managers of the responsibilities they bear for the workplace performance of the course participants. This is a dual responsibility with commissioning organisations to provide appropriate support through team meetings, staff supervision and incident reviews, and also includes monitoring the use of physical interventions. Managers need to acquire enough understanding of the subject to fulfil their responsibilities effectively, and it is advisable that they also undergo training.

5.2 Trainers are responsible for the following areas of course organisation:

- teaching practical physical intervention techniques in the context of a broader proactive management of aggressive and violent behaviours. This will include:

  - the legal context for the use of physical intervention
  - staff awareness, attitudes and values
  - a review of good practice in the use of physical intervention strategies

- the importance of positive behaviour support
- the importance of risk assessment in relation to target behaviours
- instruction in the use of selected techniques
- post-incident support for all those involved in incidents of physical intervention, that may include debriefing
- the process of recording, reporting, monitoring and evaluating physical intervention procedures employed
- provision of opportunities to practice and consolidate skills
- an individualised approach to self-assessment

- organising training courses that will provide opportunities for participants with varying experience and learning abilities to:

  - explore their own and others' attitudes to challenging behaviour and behaviour management
  - learn about and discuss the principles underlying the safe use of physical interventions
  - explore their own attitudes to the use of force with individuals, including their own right to take reasonable, lawful actions in self-defence

- making course participants aware that they have a duty to report the following to the appropriate authorities:

  - observed inappropriate sexual behaviour such as inappropriate physical contact
  - indications of the mistreatment of people using the services
  - poor performance in terms of skills, knowledge or attitudes required for the safe use of physical interventions

- organising at least one refresher course of not less than one day's duration for each successful course participant. Best practice would be annual updates or refresher courses 12 months (and not exceeding 15 months) from the date of the initial training

5.3 Courses for trainers, that take place over a considerably longer period, will be made available to applicants who have:

- agreed to abide by the BILD Code of Practice
- satisfactorily completed an introductory training course as outlined in section 5.2
- undertaken appropriate work-based experience involving the prevention and management of challenging behaviour
- have formal approval from both their employing organisation and the prospective training organisation

5.4 Aspiring trainers should be assessed in a training context and demonstrate their competence as instructors in the following:

- the ability to lead and take safe control of a training course
- detailed knowledge of the obligations imposed by the BILD Code of Practice
- the skills necessary to deliver comprehensive theory content linked to practice
- an understanding of the process of participant assessment
- the ability to provide effective feedback to participants as part of the learning process

6 Monitoring performance

6.1 The performance of each participant should be evaluated and recorded in respect of each part of the course. Areas to be included are:

- attitudes as reflected in the language and behaviour used during the course
- knowledge of appropriate positive behaviour management strategies
- knowledge of the principles underpinning the safe use of physical interventions
- competence in each practical technique taught

6.2 Each physical intervention system should establish assessment criteria and a rationale for every practical technique taught within its courses. Criteria should include:

- application of the technique
- understanding of the relevant safety principles and issues relating to risk
- gradient approaches to physical interventions

6.3 Participants who do not reach the required standard of the course should be referred and given advice and support. They should be encouraged to undertake the training at a future date where possible.

6.4 The trainer or training organisation should provide employers with feedback on the performance of each course participant.

6.5 Participants who fail to reach the required standard, and their managers, should be provided with feedback regarding:

- the areas in which they have failed to achieve competence
- the actions that can be taken to achieve competence in these areas
- the implications of their current level of competence when working with individuals who present challenging behaviour

6.6 Training organisations with trainers working under their auspices have additional responsibilities in respect of monitoring the competence of these trainers and the records they are required to maintain. The training organisations should:

- maintain a record of trainers permitted to use the organisation's name or offer a type of training promoted by that organisation
- require trainers to maintain a record of each course
- carry out a regular and systematic audit of all training records, both its own and those of its trainers, to ensure they comply with evaluation and record keeping requirements under section 7 of the Code of Practice
- provide regular opportunities for trainers to maintain and update their knowledge and skills
- ensure all trainers update their skills every 12 to 15 months

6.7 Commissioning organisations that arrange training on their own premises also have additional responsibilities. These are to:

- offer opportunities for trainers to maintain and develop their skills through regular practice opportunities with other trained staff
- ensure trainers are afforded the time to prepare and deliver training in line with the standards set out in the BILD Code of Practice

- ensure training takes place in a suitable environment
- ensure that trainers update their skills every 12 to 15 months
- keep a record of all training of trainers

7 Evaluation and record keeping

7.1 A complete record of each course should be maintained and retained by both the training and commissioning organisations for a period of not less than seven years. This record should cover:

- the nature of the course, including content, duration and trainers involved
- details of the organisation purchasing training
- the name and workplace address of each course participant, plus his or her employer organisation
- a record of health issues and physical status disclosed by any participant that might compromise their ability to participate in training
- details of participants who satisfactorily completed the course and demonstrated competence and those who did not
- action taken in respect of participants who failed to demonstrate competence
- details of all injuries or accidents reportable under health and safety legislation occurring during the training, in compliance with Reporting of Injuries, Diseases and Dangerous Occurrences Regulations (HSE)
- details of all incidents in which the usual safety guidelines were breached
- arrangements for follow-up support
- arrangements for refresher training
- details of when refresher training takes place
- details of members of the original course who attended refresher training
- participant evaluation of the course, including comments on whether the course fulfilled its stated aims and met the training needs. Any concerns about the conduct or values of trainers or fellow participants should also be retained.

7.2 Each training organisation should maintain records regarding:

- details of trainers who they currently recognise, or have previously recognised, as competent to provide training
- the standards against which the competence of trainers is measured
- the procedures employed to ensure trainers continue to meet these standards
- details of courses that have been provided by each trainer, including details of course participants
- reports of any injuries to staff or individuals who use services subsequent to training courses, for example when follow-up support is requested

7.3 Each training organisation is responsible for ensuring that its trainers maintain complete, accurate, and up-to-date records as set out in 7.1 above.

7.4 Training organisations must ensure that their recording systems comply with the Data Protection Act 1998.

8 Professional conduct

8.1   Each trainer and training organisation should undertake to maintain high standards of professional conduct. This involves:

- training staff to work in the best interests of the people who use services
- commitment to a set of core values as outlined in *Physical Interventions: A Policy Framework*
- adherence to the Code of Practice set out in this document and to the requirements of the BILD accreditation scheme
- adherence to *Guidance for Restrictive Physical Interventions*
- adherence to the *NMC Code of Conduct,* the *General Social Care Council Code of Conduct* and any other appropriate professional code
- maintenance of up-to-date knowledge of the law as it relates to the rights of children, people with a learning disability and other relevant vulnerable groups, and compliance with this law
- taking appropriate action to identify and exclude trainers who might normally be prevented from working with vulnerable persons under statutory provision
- only undertaking training for which the appropriate experience, qualifications and expertise are held
- working with other trainers and relevant statutory and voluntary bodies to improve knowledge and promote best practice
- working towards attaining BILD accreditation for training in physical interventions
- working towards a robust system of regulation for those involved in delivering training in physical interventions
- establishment of agreed approaches towards organisations and individuals who fail to meet the standards set out in this Code of Practice

- supporting other trainers
- providing independent and objective expert advice to outside bodies, including the courts
- ensuring that all public announcements, including advertising, are accurate and not liable to misinterpretation; this applies to the type of training provided, its content, quality or likely impact on staff or those who use services

Appendix: Guidance for mainstream schools that commission training

A.1 All settings, including schools, should be aware of the need to develop preventive strategies to manage challenging behaviours for pupils with learning disabilities, autistic spectrum conditions, special educational needs or behavioural, emotional and social difficulties.

A.2 It is important for staff, pupils and governors that these strategies emanate from well-thought-out policies, with support plans containing a gradient of preventive measures to diffuse difficult situations.

A.3 Staff and governors owe a duty of care to all pupils and this sometimes means that physical intervention may be appropriate to safeguard both staff and children. This should only be used in the context of agreed support plans and in conjunction with the current legislative framework (*Guidance for Restrictive Physical Interventions*, DfES/DoH July 2002). Physical intervention should only ever be used as a last resort.

A.4 It is important that staff have access to appropriate training in order to put the agreed policies and plans into practice when necessary. Such training should have an emphasis on behavioural and classroom management techniques and aim to give staff the confidence to deal with challenging behaviours without physical intervention.

A.5 It is hoped that access to BILD accredited training will have the following benefits:

- provide a safe environment for effective teaching to take place because trained staff feel empowered to use de-escalation strategies
- reduce inappropriate handling and place emphasis on creating a positive learning environment
- reduce pupil exclusions

A.6 It is acknowledged that releasing staff for training may present difficulties because of the large number involved and the potential cost. These difficulties may be overcome through releasing targeted staff who teach identified pupils with challenging behaviour. Other staff, senior managers and governors should also undergo some awareness training to maintain the holistic approach to behaviour management.

Refresher training to maintain staff skills may have to be the subject of individual school negotiation with training providers although it should meet the standards laid out in the BILD Code of Practice.

References

Allen, D. (2001) *Training Carers in Physical Interventions – Research towards evidence-based practice* Kidderminster: BILD

Allen, D. (Ed) (2002) *Ethical Approaches to Physical Interventions* Kidderminster: BILD

Allen, D. and Tynan, H. (2000) 'Responding to Aggressive Behaviour: the Impact of Training on Staff Knowledge and Confidence' *Mental Retardation* 38, 97–104

BILD (2005) *Accreditation Handbook* Kidderminster: BILD

Centre for Residential Child Care (1997) *Clear Expectations, Consistent Limits – Good Practice in the Care and Control of Children and Young People in Residential Care* Glasgow: CRCC

Department for Constitutional Affairs (2005) *Mental Capacity Act 2005* (Part 1, Section 6)

Department for Constitutional Affairs and Department of Health (awaiting publication) *Mental Capacity Act – A Code of Practice*

Department for Education and Employment (1998) Section 550a of the Education Act 1996: *The Use of Force to Control or Restrain Pupils* Circular 10/98 London: HMSO

Department of Health (1993) *Guide on Permissible Forms of Control in Children's Residential Care*

Department of Health *National Minimum Standards for Children's Homes, Residential Special Schools and Care Homes for Adults (aged 18–65)*

Department of Health (2000) *No Secrets: Guidance on Developing and Implementing Multi-Agency Policies and Procedures to Protect Vulnerable Adults from Abuse*

Department of Health (2004) *Children Act 2004* London: OPSI formerly HMSO

Department of Health (1991) *Children Act 1989 Guidance and Regulations* Vol 4 Residential Care London: HMSO

Department of Health (1995) *Children (Scotland) Act 1995* London: OPSI

Department of Health (2001) *A Safer Place: Combating Violence against Social Care Staff – Report of the National Task Force and National Action Plan* Brighton: Pavilion

Department of Health (2001) *A Safer Place: Employee Checklist – Combating Violence against Social Care Staff* Brighton: Pavilion

Department of Health and Department for Education and Skills (2002) *Guidance for Restrictive Physical Interventions – How to provide safe services for people with Learning Disabilities and Autistic Spectrum Disorder*

Department of Health and Welsh Office (1999) *Mental Health Act 1983 Code of Practice* London: HMSO

Emerson, E. (2000) Treatment and Management of Challenging Behaviour in Residential Settings *Journal of Applied Research in Intellectual Disabilities* 13 (4), 197–215

Harris, J., Allen, D., Cornick, M., Jefferson, A. and Mills, R. (1996) *Physical Interventions: A Policy Framework* Kidderminster: BILD

Health and Safety Executive (1999) *Reporting of Injuries Diseases and Dangerous Occurrences Regulations*

Health and Safety Executive (1997) *First Aid at Work: Your Questions Answered*

Home Office (1998) *Speaking up for Justice:* Home Office Justice and Victims Unit

Lyon, C. (1994) *Legal Issues arising from the Care Control and Safety of Children with Learning Disabilities who also present with Severe Challenging Behaviour* London: Mental Health Foundation

Lyon, C. and Pimor, A. (2004) *Physical Interventions and the Law* Kidderminster: BILD

Mental Welfare Commission for Scotland (2001) *Rights, Risks and Limits to Freedom*

National Institute of Mental Health (2004) *Developing Positive Practice to Support the Safe and Therapeutic Management of Aggression and Violence in Mental Health In-patient Settings*

NHS Executive (2000) *We Don't Have to Take This: NHS Zero Tolerance Zone* London: Department of Health

Office of Public Sector Information *Mental Capacity Act 2005*

Scottish Institute for Residential Child Care (2005) *Holding Safely: A Guide For Residential Care Practitioners and Managers about Physically Restraining Children and Young People*

The Scottish Executive (2000) *Standards in Scottish School Act 2000*

The Scottish Executive (2000) *Better Behaviour, Better Learning*

The Scottish Executive (2004) *Education (Additional Support for Learning) (Scotland) Act 2004*

The Scottish Executive (2005) *Supporting Children's Learning – Code of Practice*

The Scottish Executive (2005) *Safe and Well: Good Practice in Schools and Education Authorities for Keeping Children Safe and Well*

The Welsh Assembly Government (2005) *Framework for Restrictive Physical Intervention Policy and Practice*

TOPSS England (2001) *The Care Training Code: Voluntary Code of Practice for Trainers of Social Care Students, Candidates and Staff, and guide for purchasers of training*

United Kingdom Central Council for Nursing, Midwifery and Health Visiting (1999) *Practitioner Client Relationships and the Prevention of Abuse*

BILD website
www.bild.org.uk